Turning the Stones

for Richard
with admiration
from
Alistair
Dec 1993

Also by Alistair Elliot from Carcanet

My Country:
Collected Poems

ALISTAIR ELLIOT
Turning the Stones

Alistair Elliot

CARCANET

Acknowledgements

I am grateful to the editors or literary editors of the following journals, in which most of these poems first appeared: *British Medical Journal, London Review of Books, London Magazine, New Statesman & Society, The Spectator, Times Literary Supplement, Poetry Review, PN Review, Poetry Wales, Verse, Rialto, Arion, Encounter, Margin, North Dakota Quarterly,* and *Spectrum*; and to the editors of the Poetry Book Society anthologies for 1986/87, 1989/90 and Volumes 1-3 of the new series; also to the editor of *High on the Walls*, the Morden Tower 25-year celebration anthology, and to the editors of *The Emissary* (Heaton Manor School, Newcastle upon Tyne).

Several of the poems were broadcast on one of Radio 3's *Living Poet* programmes.

'At Appleby Horse Fair' won the Prudence Farmer Award for 1991.

First published in 1993 by
Carcanet Press Limited
208-212 Corn Exchange Buildings
Manchester M4 3BQ

A CIP catalogue record for this book
is available from the British Library.
ISBN 1 85754 041 7

The publisher acknowledges financial assistance
from the Arts Council of Great Britain

Set in 10pt Times by Bryan Williamson, Frome, Somerset
Printed and bound in England by SRP Ltd, Exeter

Contents

The Walk

We may see nothing here some days,
but the walk itself is rich. In one place

the ghost of a fox, with a bad leg,
comes into focus. A rabbit sits and begs,

entirely remembered. We can watch
hoverflies, living, dead, or not yet hatched,

and call on a hole beside a sycamore
where a bumblebee lived alone in '84.

Ten years ago we saw a hare
thinking in that dull field: it's still there,

and somewhere among those chestnuts are eight herons
in a high wind trying to keep their balance.

Near the beginning of the wood
we always pause and listen, where we stood

hearing an invisible giant, thrashing leaves
and closing fast; in danger of our lives

we stood our ground, until a tiny world
like dust from under a bed blew onto the path and twirled;

then others even smaller, squeaking,
crossed the worn earth and crashed in the grass, still talking.

I have forgotten you; and even you. But they,
it seems, are kept. Cannot be thrown away.

A Memorial Service

The cathedral was not great.
You were a better poet
Than it was a building. I forgot
To look for the graffiti of imprisoned Scots,
My possible ancestors – and yours –
And stood there in my Sunday best
Wondering if it had been spoilt by the restorers
Or if it had always looked like red fudge
A little mouthed by the weather of the north-west.

Hundreds of us were in our best
To honour you – ties added in haste
In the graveyard where we stood
Chin up, in Peter Rabbit's attitude,
While our companions' fingers adjusted the knot.
It might have been some consolation for dying,
If you had needed any, and perhaps not
(Weren't you a Christian?), to see how many, strange
Or famous, had given you their evening.

Limp ties, or stiff necks, something insincere
Can spoil these timed explosions of honour.
Not this time – it was the glory-encrusted bishop
Who made it natural: his hair stuck up
Behind, as disobedient as a boy's.
The choristers came chanting up the aisle,
He followed: you'd have laughed to see the eyes
Of the mothers spot that tuft, and waver, and exchange
With other women a complicated smile.

Inflation

What happened to the money
laid out for perpetual masses
in the Middle Ages? The souls
astonished and half-free
from the pains of purgatory
wonder what their obols,
crowns, half-crowns and angels
were spent on. Repairing gargoyles
and whitening surplices?
Re-staining time-pale glass?

Having put down enough
to flood the town with beer,
dress everyone for miles
in silk, and buy love
for the unkind and rough,
they find the daily silence
a horribly painful puzzle –
stuck, as they are, to the gills
in penitential fire:
what has happened to prayer?

Could the earth have been destroyed?
they are asking, as they turn
in the grave sarabande
of torment, grilled and flayed.
Can it possibly be that God
has changed the rate of payment
for mortgaged souls, or even
merged the places of punishment
and raised the price of heaven?
Or are we just forgotten?

MCMVI

In Memoriam James Adam Elliot, MD ChB (Edinburgh)
Glencoul, August 1901 – Clatterbridge, August 1991

The postman used to shout across the loch
till they rowed over. Once it was for Will,
from Carnegie. 'He's somewhere on the hill
getting our dinner. Who's this Carnegie?' 'Rich.'

Will was fifteen, the eldest, trying to teach
my father (five) his letters. In Glencoul
their lonely house was technically a school.
Their textbook might have been the Pentateuch.

Carnegie offered a fiver and a bookcase
for the School Library. So when Will came back
with the pony, the muzzle-loader and a carcase,
the boys composed a letter. They sent the cheque
to a bookshop, with two clippings from the *Herald*:
Everyman's Library Classics a Shilling Each,
and someone's Hundred Best Books of the World.
They'd fetch them in the boat, from Kyle, next week.

The boys have disappeared: the teacher, Will,
in France, of the same plague as Pericles;
my namesake died when No-Man threw a shell;
my father, of Medea's skin disease.

The books may well survive. The one I'd like,
perhaps on a tray in the rain now, marked '10p',
is *Vanity Fair*, in which the boy got stuck
half up the tree of knowledge. I would look
for the words he read, to everybody's glee,
'He was a man of charming gravy-tea.'

Highland Hospitality

When the two youngest Elliots,
not yet in their teens,
were sent to school at Stoer,
they lodged, like the unmarried minister,
near the kirk, with old Mrs Mackenzie
and her daughters
in a house called 'The Rage of the Cats'.

Mrs Mackenzie fed them porridge
and milk; potatoes and milk
and oatcakes; perhaps a bite
of potatoes and herring...
This powered them through four hours of Gaelic
on Sundays; but even the man in black
must have prayed for colour in the diet.

At kirk, strangers would shake their hands,
thank them, and recall their father's house.
These dark-clothed men were herring-fishers
who in the eighties, even the seventies,
had followed the shoals from the Minch
through the narrows at Kylesku
and on, up the dark loch, Glendhu.

There they would spread their nets at dusk
and a sail among the rocks:
opposite, the boys' future father
left his house open, the table set
with land meat and a fire lit,
and sometimes didn't wait up. What an idea!
To be his guests and not see him!

The boys could not explain the Rage of Cats,
but now we understand
the name on the map where the path is lost
among boulders, Carn Sgadan:
Cairn of Herrings, monument
to the fish, the shy dark men,
the bounty of the past.

Revisiting the American Museum of Natural History

The large domed hall is dim as memory,
with set scenes off it like shop-windows. There
we once stood, looking out – one bright small room
still shows a plain with buffaloes; the same mother
keeps guard, watching the distance while her young,
already killed and stuffed, gambol around.

We wondered how they died. I still wonder
forty years later. Next we looked at Old
New York – or rather old New Amsterdam.
Here, they show human dead – not stuffed, just models –
with Peg-Leg Pete the Governor (Stuyvesant)
hearing a delegation from some Indians.

He turns a half-cheek, like Dick Tracy, standing
outside his house at No. 1, Broadway.
At ten I didn't see, but now I notice
the soldier with the flintlock is his brother:
they have the same cheek – and he's also twins
with the Hackensacks, the warriors who stand listening.

All men were brothers, in the forties. Seriously?
Was that a wartime feeling? The designer,
more likely, only had one mould for features.
But the faces of the squaws behind are different –
his moulds could make two species, men and women.
They slant across the background: they are bowing

to keep their carry-bands firm on their brows
and brace their baskets, so no corn is lost.
Opposite, a settler's wife leans in a doorway,
so badly dressed you'd think her clothes were stolen.
The squaws, their lovely milk-places bare, wait for a
small boy or a premature photographer.

This might have been the year after Pearl Harbor,
when I recalled my mother's chest as flat.
For I had lost that figure of a mother
in a terrible dream: for weeks she crossed the Atlantic,
the shivering bosom of winter, with lads named Johann
and Wolfgang steady underwater hunting.

Turning away, I see the long-forgotten
Protozoa: another refugee
from the Old World had blown them, selves without parents,
in glass. I could be envious of these spheres,
rowing so variously round the globe –
the food of everyone, or future marble.

Their rounded symmetry strikes me as a blessing,
the perfect shape, according to a Greek
fed by a breast. Do they have memories,
packed in the single cell? And do they hunger
as we do, for the cells that peel away,
buoyed up in something warm and watery?

On Broadway

There are some small shops left. The name
over the door was half a physics textbook.
A little bell announced me. I began
by showing that my watch, or time itself,
had worn away its strap, the animal skin
that holds the disc of Chronos where I see it.

The man was older than me, and grey
where I am reddish, the pommettes not ripened
by glances of the sun: a prisoner
of commerce in his twilit glass-walled cell,
spied on all day by the faces of unsold watches.
I found his straps too dear, and shyly said so:

'You see, I live by writing verse.
One poem beds and boards me for two days,
but who can write a poem every day,
or every other?' He was a poet too,
but not for money. We compared our work:
'I write about the cost of watch-straps.' He wrote

on German concentration camps.
'When I was twelve, my father had me taught
to understand the works of watches: people
would always want to know the time. One day
we were all arrested. After that, I fixed
the broken watches in twenty-one different death-camps.'

Few can have made so grand a tour
of infamous places. Should I have enquired
about his horrible itinerary?
I could imagine him in small bureaux
returning life to fine machines, alone,
unable to enquire about the customers.

'The commandants transferred me like
a football-player; I earned my life, but not
my father's or my mother's or the others'...'
He made me take a sixteen-dollar strap
for nothing. We shook hands, for one moment
Landau & Elliot, the old firm, family poets.

A Family Wireless

You switch it on, pour out a cup of tea,
drink it, and finally sounds of outer space
clearing its throat blow from the vizored face;
pause; then the swelling voice of history
refills our kitchen from the B.B.C.

I daren't re-tune it: set before the war
on Home, it doesn't know it's Radio Four.
It never knew the Third, or Radio Three.
It had the Light, but mostly what has stained
the mouth-like patch there on the gauze was news:

Achilles, Ajax, Exeter have passed
from there into my head; six million gassed;
and eighty million others –
                                        Old friend, amuse
us now: what recent victories have we gained?

Miss Vermilion

Should teachers be like us
or beautifully different? I was ten
and would have married Miss Vermilion.
Her scarlet lips blew, not kisses
but knowledge toward me for a year,
and I remember none of it, only her.

Or rather, I admit, I must be carrying
somewhere her words: *improper fraction*
perhaps, *militia*, or *Des Moines*,
in the string-bag of my vocabulary,
but smeared so thin across the neurones
there's no retrieval of the names of donors.

I would like to thank her, if she is human
somewhere still, not dark or slim
now, but lovely as once, in the shaded schoolroom –
mysterious giver, like those ancient women
whose babies gave a soul
to a new bridge, or voice to a village bell.

Learning to Swim

My swimming teacher in Palm Beach
was on the American team
at the Berlin Olympics.
No naked prince was ever so handsome!
He taught the children of the very rich –
and a few others – how to kick
and how to breathe between strokes.
I think he was killed in the Pacific.

Back in England, when I saw my father
doing the breast-stroke (as I thought),
I circumnavigated him
like a shark patrolling a boat,
all elbows and yawning mouth.
His arms rowed backwards in great swathes;
his eyes bugged out; he grinned. What a scream,
I thought, in our open-air baths

which looked like Fort Zinderneuf.
'In the Highlands nobody swam. We learned from frogs,'
he tells me now; 'up the col
on Craig Glas they live in a bit of bog.
We'd take them down to the Glencoul River
and imitate them.' I wish I'd had such lessons –
three boys in a salmon pool
with their unhappy *professeurs de natation*...

The Cord

The little creature flies
or floats in the liberties
of its mother's body,
kicking from side to side of
its narrow round-edged pool
like a fish, or a kite that tries
the depth of its small warm sky
with a thoughtful pull
at the end of its tether,
the line that goes to earth.

If anything breaks that line
you can float free, down
an automatic wind
with freedom to fall to the end;
but if you survive, always
you will need to find the like
again, a string of looks
that tethers you to a face,
to the curve from which you depend,
to the dry warmth of a hand.

Meetings

I think the soft blue ghost
of a baby you had lost
hung over our first meeting.
I was invited to talk,
to be a stranger and distracting,
but neither of us spoke.

I remember the Russian icons
cut from magazines
and glued on cheap black wood.
I remember the apple trees
behind the semi, the unmowed
grass lapping our knees.

I saw your beauty then
as you stepped into the garden.
But now I see what courage
you must have had, to face us
with your tray of cremated sausage,
bare, in that thin sad dress.

This time you're wearing trousers,
and offer a plate of samosas,
and look pregnant. But this
re-alignment of lips is not
a smile but a goodbye kiss.
This growth will take you with it:

You have begun to slide,
in your oriental bed,
towards your last birth.
But how easily we talk! –
of your young hand; of earth
you will soon be salting; of some book.

More Swimming

Now I remember standing in the pool
myself, a Baptist, teaching you the crawl
without touching, my hand
hovering under your navel
like a poacher's. Dear lost pupil,
if I had grasped you then,
it might have been an ordinary hand
earthing the wet and non-conductive skin.

But I lay down beside you
like a husband, and began to swim,
to show the commotion of legs,
and how water is caught in the arms.
And afterwards I fed you
my foreign fish-paste, my rye bread,
unrecognized smells of sex
in the innocent hand and head.

We did not know that we were naked
under our damp clothes
to each other. It was later
that we put words in each other's mouths
instead of food,
and then it was as if, instead of coming
out of the water to mate, we
lay on the grass and continued swimming.

The Scribes

More and more often, knowing that you're dying,
I think of the letter-writers at the post-office
in that hot square, with their low desks and dip-pens
waiting in the shade of their municipal trees
for the illiterate victims of time and distance –
the dealers in words, renewing or untying.

Whenever I passed them I would think of paying
to have my raw wish wrapped in the empty nets
of their professional calligraphy,
the well-rubbed language of a thousand nights,
and always hesitated ('how could she
know what these frightening loops and spikes were saying?').

I should have paid, and risked your sitting crying
in your own post-office, half-wanting to laugh
at this incomprehensible world of effort.
But how could I foresee our separate lives? –
and the need for something kept from the fire, a comfort
framed on the wall, a cause of shrugs and smiling,

diploma from another way of lying:
those syllables, formed by someone with the tip
of his tongue just showing, would say *I love you* (formal),
I love you (intimate) over your throne-of-sleep –
where you no longer   (verb used only by female)
between the Indian coverlet and the domes of silence.

The Love of Horses

The lost people of Atlantis must have sent us
This weather, full of dying breaths.
The horses add to it, panting as we climb
The tearful slope;
So do the formally lamenting sheep,
Who miss their lambs and know who is to blame.

I'm on a highland garron, disgraceful Caesar
Whom everyone loves: a steaming nicotine-
Stained character with a black mane
And a humorous stolid look,
The sort that always tries to be last in line
But runs up hills with a dead weight on his back.

The fields were terraced by the people of Calroust
In the Middle Ages, and later walled. One field
Stops us; we cannot pass, because
It holds a mare and foal. In fact, the mare
Has already singled out my Caesar,
Hung her head over the wall and met his eyes.

Solemn, they haven't noticed we too are silent,
To watch the very gentle slow approach
Of the two flaring noses;
Putting their long thin faces side by side
They discreetly snuff each other's essences.
This taking of breath – what could be more polite?

In a trance of unfamiliar fumes, they dream
(Looking judiciously over each other's shoulder)
On the art of overlapping forms,
On the truthfulness of odours, the grace of necks,
Round haunches, crooked legs, and have just reached
The aching loneliness of farms,

When Helen says cheerily, 'Oh he's such a Lothario,
Caesar – but she's a thoroughbred and in season.
We'll have to go round.' I thought the mare
Knew a good horse when she smelled one. On we trot,
Thinking he might not ever again smell her.
That small rain from Atlantis tangs of salt.

The Use of Knees

Everyone calls it Arthuritis. He
has lost the power of bending, the old king
father of gods and men,
and sits on a low throne
by the window, apparently meditating
in profile, a memorial coin
of sadness as we come carrying our seats.

To me he has never before been Arthur:
I saw him through his unused name,
so fitting for a father
born in a Scottish Eden: Adam.
Caught in the unfamiliar foetal posture
of a bronze age burial,
he tries to uncurl and honour us with a smile.

Of course he is 'not so dusty'; so he says
when asked, but still his legs,
locked at a regal angle under the gown,
or under sheets, abruptly evoke a coffin
humped in the middle like this eiderdown,
or a succession of little hammer breaks
flattening the folded sediments of those knees.

He will have thought of that. He will
already know how undertakers solve
mortal geometry, keeping calm themselves.
And maybe such a man has even seen
himself finally dusty, and me on the hill
kneeling, releasing the native dust between
Corriekinloch and the sand of Loch an Eircill.

At Appleby Horse Fair

The young men stand in the River Eden
half-naked, splashing and washing their horses
to sell up there on the skyline,
but also parading
themselves, their thin teenage torsos,
their skeletons hardly hidden, their red skin.

Barefoot on the bed of the stony river
in soaking trousers, they appear to
be doing just as they want:
shouting unintelligible
words which then they squirt on
pinto backsides in green detergent.

But when the ponies regain their colours,
the lads shorten their grasp on a headrope,
jump on a back, and file
off up the hill in silence.
Selling your friends is a hard job;
it helps to do it with style.

Shagbags

In those half-innocent days
we looked at each other's eyes
each morning: a purple bruise
betrayed one had helped himself
to a handful of grown-up life,
and we began to tease.

We looked with awe at girls
who wore the dark half-circles
of happiness like medals,
proud of their well-spent hours
in the arms, and legs, of others,
adventures a woman conceals.

We tried in vain to imagine
the play of limbs and skin,
the fingers trailed on a brown
smoothness that furrows like water,
with radar-rings of pleasure
pulsing from zone to zone.

It never occurred to us
that the stains of sleeplessness
might not be daubed by a penis;
that the black upturned rainbows
or growth-rings beside the nose
come from a world of causes.

Still when I see these signs
I forget the sadder reasons.
The rumour of adolescence
comes back: the tender bruise
of time preserved, from days
otherwise left in ruins.

Un Coeur Simple

When I arrived in London
to set a trap or two for fortune,
I got a job in Covent Garden,
as a vegetable invoice clerk.
It earned me seven pounds a week.
That was a marvellous place to work...
Now there's a restaurant ('The African Cook')

next door, but then a saveloy stall
fed the market porters and the retail
greengrocers and the odd gent in tails.
The Communist Party's offices
were near, probably bombed, rebuilt with those
translucent bricks they used to use
in the ceilings of public lavatories:

a glass house where sideways was up.
The other way was the opera,
needing paint but much more popular –
people at least went in and out.
At lunch I'd walk to the Charing Cross Road
shops for a book, or south
to watch the Thames flow back, or forth.

Of course this was before
you could see the National Theatre
and its sign, or catch my dear
sunbathing on the leads of Somerset House –
I just liked river views,
and probably confused
Wordsworth's bridge with Waterloo's.

The work was turning bills
for toms, mush, daffodils,
sniffables and edibles,
into invoices and envelopes.
Sometimes we got so bored we'd heap
our desks with crumpled scraps,
for indoor bonfires of papers.

One day I recall I brought a
novel by an American author
born the year before my grandfather –
I think it was *The Portrait
of a Lady*, or maybe *The Awkward
Age* – and a man there (who looked like Robert
Louis Stevenson but older) had actually met him.

'What happened?' 'Well, I was very
young indeed. I gave your hero a daisy –'
'And what did he wonderfully say?'
'He inclined his great clean smiling head
down to me, shook my hand, and uttered
the inescapable two words
even the greatest use for gratitude.'

Homer

My wife, the savage one with the savage name,
has gone today to meet Homer. I imagine
that relaxed ghost drifting into the lesson
to mouth his own nearly-forgotten phonemes.

What will she lip-read first? ANDRA? – the MAN
who turned his hand to anything, who could come
in the bed of a witch, then stubbornly sail home
to his Greek wife over the OINOPA PONTON?

Or will he sigh, turning the leaves, of ANGER,
MÊNIN, the tearing of the social net,
that makes the gods behave like men, and HEROES
refuse their definition: BORN TO FIGHT?

'Homer,' I shout: 'beyond all this, remind her
is the GIFT OF SLEEP and RHODODAKTULOS ÊÔS.'

Cornelia

Somewhere beyond the Tigris – or the Euphrates –
a Parthian gripped his horse between his knees,
turned in the saddle, shot: and you became
a widow silently, in range in Rome.

Later you would have cried – young Crassus' face
never to join the gallery of imagos –
and counted back: Lucretius' posthumous book
was possibly in your hands when the arrow struck.

After some months your father offered you
to Pompey: chaste, well-read and beautiful widow.
He had been married to Caesar's daughter – who died,
was it in childbirth, a child with a big head?

For Pompey was big: you would have learnt success
in battle from him, manoeuvering round a kiss,
turning his flank. He made your father consul;
and wondering why, you began to be political.

Why did Caesar have to come back from Gaul?
It gave you a drive through Italy, and a sail
to Lesbos, where you would be safe – and lonely.
What was there then to do in Mytilene? –

while Venus came and went, the precious coins
of marriage wasted, waiting in the distance.
It seems you crossed to Pergamon, where they liked you
and honoured you 'for your kindness' with a statue.

It's dust now. What were you like? Our only clue is
that you apologized for Pharsalus
to Pompey, when he finally came, in a caique:
'Your fortune has been spoiled by my bad luck.'

How many weeks were left? You must have felt,
not many, sailing off – and all your fault –
without a destination. When he stepped
into the little boat to land in Egypt,

you tried to stop him. How awful to be proved
right as you watched the body you had loved
stabbed there, and there, and have no remedy.
His head was cut off as you sailed away.

In time his ashes with their dreadful question –
how much is here? – caught up with you. By then
you knew you were still childless. You retired,
not to inflict your fortune on a third

unfortunate, into the dark of history –
which looks like death, from here. But somebody
surely said in your hearing three years later:
'Caesar died at the foot of Pompey's statue.'

No more is known. No epitaph. Dolabella,
and worse men still, 'improved' your Alban villa.
I hope you lived to read the marvellous poets
who sang as the Republic fell to bits.

Alfred Ernout

What happened to Ernout?
He edited Plaute,
it seemed the thing to do
at the time, I guess he'd say.
In 1932
(the year my parents gave each other me)
his mind was on the illegitimate son
of Alcmène et Amphitryon;
'The Donkey One'; and
'Something to Do with Flutes' –
three plays whose titles start with A.

I suppose he'd thought:
I'm glad to be alive
after the war, and Plautus makes me laugh,
with his ingenious slaves and stupid soldiers,
and sons cheating their fathers
so as to pay for whores
who turn out to be sisters, cousins or daughters.
If he could write it in the Punic Wars,
as it were between glaciers,
then I can edit it in time of peace.
Plautus and Plutus never shared an address,
but it might happen yet, if I say yes.

So he began this comic work, and I
became a serious-looking boy
called by my godfather –
who'd been on walking tours along the Rhine –
Hans Fritz von Spekulator.
Our holidays were in Scotland, though:
one summer, in Glendhu,
I remember seeing Mrs Chamberlain
and her children on the hill, too shy
to ask my aunt for a cup of tea.
Her husband was off-stage, probably
begging his tea from some dictator.

Ernout meanwhile was more or less
at 'Poenulus', where a rather nice
Carthaginian tidies up the mess.
Plautus writes a speech for him
in Punic, full of words that end in *im*
and *ith* and *ot*.
Old soldiers in the audience would love that.

Outside the study, Peace
had put on battledress
to keep warm: those old glaciers
were grinding south toward his living-room,
and like the fellow in the final volume
he had to ask: What shall I do?

How should I spend
the minutes we have left before the end?
The coins of life are few.
In 1938
Tomes V and VI came out.
That was his answer to the vital doubt.

Our answer was not quite the same.
It's true that when the war began
I began Latin –
but so did everyone
aged six (or seven) in England then.
I was just drifting down the stream.
My parents saw the ice or gas ahead.
They started writing to their friends abroad:
'You say you want our children?'

Here is Tome VII in my hand. See,
they finished printing, on this paper, all
the rest of Plautus, every syllable
that has survived, clean or dirty,
in Antwerp on a Thursday,
the 25th of April,
1940.

Two weeks later,
the Germans invaded,
and – as I saw,
safe in a cinema in America –
the roads filled up with refugees,
lorries and carts, carrying away
the idea of home, carpets
and children, beds and tables, and these sheets
of Latin literature,
to the dark shops of fallen Paris,

where Professor Ernout
was working on his new
parallel-text Lucretius –
which he brought out discreetly
some time in 1942.

Talking to Ronnie Tylecote

Dear Ronnie, you have gone before
to the place I think is empty,
the corridors of nowhere.
I think I address your memory when I say,
'Wait for us there'
in the uncomfortable hammocks
that gravity hangs from star to star:
we want your company when we explore
the furnaces of the galaxy.

You were the one we wanted here
on the planet of war –
not as a fighter, free distributor
of heavy patiently dug-up objects and fire,
but for afterwards, to begin again
in the stripped hills with finding ore,
then to explain
how to get iron out of a stone,
and how to beat it
into a fish-hook and a strong frying-pan.
Men should know metals; and you did.

You knew the military keenness
of certain elements: their wish to link in
regular ranks and companies,
to shine, or ring with a single
uninflected unanimous voice.
You also knew the histories
of making: we could join,
we could rejoin with your advice
at the easiest place
the cultural procession.

Here you would smile
('the cultural procession'
which goes backwards so often)
and as you used to do when we dropped by,
pick up a sock, pretend to darn it,
teasing us all,
the scientist as a boy –
while everybody wondered if you'd worn it

with your own heel
or with the other (metal) one.

For you were the perfect
example of your strangely cold subject –
the warm metallurgist
with a tin leg to stand on.
You were the man who took
my wife to *The Seraglio*
(was that your joke?)
and in the bar enthused
not about the opera,
but the alloy
in the new cans of beer.

You were the man who flew
thousands of miles to see
the slag-heaps of Meroe
far up the Nile,
the Bronze Age smelting-hearth at Timna
in Israel,
the Phoenician silver-mines in Spain,
even the Scottish antimony mine
where my great-grandfather was born.

Archaeologists dig
for the rubbish of the past:
that is their treasure, a man-made thing
of interest in the chronological waste.
Your treasure was the slag
or oddly small stone building
left by an illiterate long ago,
who knew something you knew,
something we did not know.

Ronnie, you taught us to read
that dross, that excrement of metal bathed
and battered by the flow of time
into a message clearer than a poem:
and when you were cremated
you went into the furnace with that leg
and a comforting handful of Greek slag.
You would have known, at that low heat,
what would survive unscathed.

Maybe we shall not meet
in that strange space
where *homo sapiens sapiens* is thought
to flit as easily as light
through absolute emptiness,

but when I read of Beowulf's helmet
flashing and fire-hard,
when I hear of uranium waste
fused with glass and encased
in Corinthian bronze, then buried
like amphorae and ingots in the ocean,
when I heft my little metal writing-spear,
then we meet here
on this encrusted ball of molten iron,
on which you lived with us and wrote
amid the slag from some exploded sun.

On the Great North Road

Here hedges used to move off
thoughtfully, at an angle,
like green sheep in single file,
or seemed to. Now they really have,
taking the grass as well,
leaving the land stripped to the buff.

What we see is pure substrate,
the abstract thing plants grow on,
the start-line of a calculation.
I think it is a dusty mat
someone has spread on the slow ocean
of rock. Is this my planet?

The wind is blowing it away.
The solid earth begins to turn
into a brown gas. A neutrino
drives through England in this way.
My eyes water, my lungs burn.
Am I allergic to my country?

Banks

The long hills of the Midlands are called banks.
There Shakespeare-lovers
Go, for wild thyme, timeflowers, bumclocks, all such wildness
As England offers.
For now it's tame enough: lovers can barely
Finish their explorations
Before whole families step blushing by,
In three generations.

My grandfather, the crowscarer, knew this differently:
He would stand guard
Each autumn while his father dug, and buried
All he was worth,
On the family walk to the workhouse for the winter.
The fields are hard
Under the fingers of the poor: old customers
In the bank of earth.

Old Bewick

We come for a day of peace: the wick
of bees, the ripples widening on a rock
scratched by fingers that never fondled iron,
the lumpy mattress of moor, with cairns for buttons,
the curves of Cheviot and marine horizons.

We learn the place was given as a reward
to a Northumbrian who killed Malcolm the Third,
Macbeth's successor: crime and death
to delight, instruct and move. We thread the gate
onto the common, dazed by northern heat.

A mile to Blawearie. Something quicker than time
and rain has broken the grey abandoned farm:
somebody has been practising war. We eat
in sycamore shade, staying under cover
when a helicopter rises and slides over.

Three fleas hang on the skyline, trailing ropes
or legs or smoke. They hide and hop
over our heads, scattering turds of sound.
The curlews have to cry a little louder
to keep a territory on the Border.

For this is still the Debatable Land. In cities,
in rooms, you can forget the competition.
Here in the heather, when our earth lies open
and the sun takes it, you feel the very ground
of fighting, the fatal impulse to defend.

A Workshop in Boulder, Colorado

The street heads toward silence
in the evening light – its straight lines
fading out before the mountains.
Here, set back, is the workshop where I think
all the darkness of this clean town has sunk:
shapes too black to see, and Merle
himself all but invisible,
pale carpenter of metal.

He is older than three ordinary
men, older than this century
of wars, and almost speechlessly shy
or tired, for today the dirty hand
he touches to mine has drawn out and machined
a mould for casting laser components in.
Some of his earlier work is on the moon;
some, on the way to Neptune.

His favourite art was the exploded pics
in *Popular Mechanix*,
and he has added to it, from the sticks
addressing the cosmopolis: his pieces
are off touring the universe.
He's happy, whether they fall
into a star, or some black hole
obscurer than this room, or sparkle
on some extraordinary collector's wall.

Ephemeroptera, Wisconsin

for Park Teter

Our brothers being imperfect – or far off –
we take rest in our friendship, as in this
canoe, impelled unsteadily over
Lake Katherine's very slightly dusty surface.
Kneeling, I remember my childhood: in my shoulder
a small memory moves, to twist the paddle.
The water speaks of its own sweetness.

We whisper too, like hunters: what we're after
is all around us. In a way
it is your Garden of Eden that we drift through,
that you visited every summer as a boy.
But somebody's fallen; for in and over the water
the mayflies mate and die, unable to eat:
this is the evening of their only day –

their only day in air. Before, of course,
they lived down there, under the bright meniscus
with sparkling planets of dust, among the spars
of gloomy plants, losing brothers and sisters
to gliding fish, and nourished on sad cells
of algae and diluted chlorophyll:
an almost completely unhelpful pre-existence.

So they come to this day as I do, ignorant
and wanting introductions: to your island,
which hooks at us with shallows, to the tamarack
by your old camp, to Hesperus, a planet
born as we turn for home, with silhouettes
of mayflies drawing up a dance, and bats
shrieking over their feast of edible sound.

These little furry spirits in their joy
exclaim so – surely this is not a useful
hunting vibration, but free expressive noise.
I am excited too and start to whistle
across the family distance. But I've said
more than a man should say to a strange bat:
they swoop, enraged – I interrupt the festival.

To them the whistle must have been a light
blinding their ears, much like unbalancing
a man in a canoe. We face the sunset
without a syllable of speech or song
and pull for home across the shining debris
of the bats' party, the fragments of dead flies.
Thanks for the lifetime, the annual meal, the evening.

Remains of Mining in the Upper Peninsula, Michigan

This was the edge of history,
the lip of the wave that licks at chaos;
and these are the first tools,
these houses glistening with the oils
of human skin, and smelling of old clothes,
genuine nineteenth-century
smoke and the powder of ancient pastry.

This raw log box
holds still, in the freshness of the forest,
the essences of miners.
At first I think the stale patina's
the taste of bachelors, the shiny crust
baked on a man by work;
but they were clean men, Finns, with a sauna by the creek.

Besides, this is the scent
of grandma's house, a reek of home
that has not chimneyed up my nose
for fifty years: I recognize,
thousands of miles away, the Model Farm,
and am no longer entirely present,
odour discrediting every other sense.

This puzzling family smell
is what my new nephew caught
when I first lifted him:
under the hinge of my arm
blew his mother's microclimate,
her musty rain-forest, with one small
difference, one less flower and one new animal.

But how do my relatives enter this?
I suddenly realize
my widening modern nostrils
are following the trail,
the cold track, of my own race:
what the shocked Indians greeted with courtesies,
the stink of white men in the wilderness.

Falling Among Minocquabats

For Diana
and her daughters

The water's almost luke
warm now, but only three months back
a small boy on a bike
could have towed me upright across the lake:
the skin of liquid offering a walk.

Now it takes a powerboat
and three stimulating ladies:
kindnesses and beauties
that pull a man to his feet
for the smallest part of a minute.

The ridge of wake like a seam
saws at my perineum,
sluicing me like a Muslim.
I shall be washed smooth as a woman
before I learn this kind of skiing!

I hardly mind if I don't learn,
I realise slowly: it's more fun
falling again and again
for you than, single-footed, planing
the ripples off Lake Katherine like your cousin.

Success must lead to boredom, I think,
swallowing another yard of drink.
When I bob up, and see you circling,
with faces straight but very kind,
your swimsuits quaking,

I think I could do this for ever –
as long as you could want. Your laughter
rings out to the changeless trees of winter,
but never quite reaches my ear
under the temporary water.

Amalfi

It was as a panorama with a moral
I saw it: a wide painting fit for Brueghel
The Elder, which I attempted (in a postcard
Lost at your death) to describe. Seen from my window
Above, the piazza was a large stone oblong
With people following purposes across it.
Top right, a family fishing, the children scaring
The catch away by swinging their white feet
Over the quayside. Nearer a man crying
The virtues of his food, a little shop
On wheels. A patient talkative queue
Waiting for boats to Capri. The bright clothes
Of almost all showed they were chorus players,
Foreigners probably, the older ones
Offering each other drinks, the younger trying
Their first shy words. The groups were well arranged
According to the rules for human distance
And covered the whole space, but, finally,
A stroke of composition brought a car
(Which formed a vee of people with its wake)
To centre stage. The driver raised the bonnet.
It burst in flames. Those who were near it made
A circle; thus, the others could not see it,
But kept on strolling here and there, and talking,
And posting nuts in open mouths, as carefully
As if in danger from their lovers' teeth.

My Brown Boots

The brown boots carried me the day before
round the temple at Bassae, and I wore
them still that evening as we sat to eat,
I at the corner of Kolokotronis Street,
you at my elbow in Odos Sophokleous.
                        You said,
          'Fuck sightseeing; fuck sightseers.
          Those Dutch girls are a day ahead,
          but we can catch their spongy rears
          and chase them into bed.'

So in the morning I shaved and put on shoes
to run for the dawn bus. The boots were loose,
not tethered to a bag, and on the bus
they slid along the floor away from us
and our intentions – oh my battered friends
of family holidays and fair weekends! –
and hid; and when the driver put us down
at a cross-roads, pointing to the ancient town
up there, above the olives, on the hill,
the boots stayed on, nudging each other, still
shuffling about their metal hiding-place.
                              Before
                    the bus was out of sight
                    I knew the boots lay on its floor,
                    trembling, open-mouthed with fright.
                    What and where were they bound for?

At the lonely kapheneion, 'Theo Ness,'
you said; 'F. Callisto. And may we shed
our pragmata here till we can find a bed
up in the polis? Know a place?' 'You stay
with Mr Kokkalopoulos, okay?'

Nice walking in the sun. A dry old land
of spicy dust we long to understand.
One should go everywhere on foot. You are
memorizing details with your camera,
while I take in a gentle climb through air
into a box of space, the village square,
a ramp to the left, a street that has a view

to the horizon – 'Look, it's Alph.' 'Alf who?'
'Zeus' favourite river' – and a donkey too,
which lives in Mr Kokkalopoulos' basement.
He lets us have a room with a French gazement
looking west, and a balcony, and informs us
along it sleep two foreigners with enormous
something that's round. 'But are they Ollandézé?'
'Tsk. Tsk.' 'We saw them on the way to Bassae;
we think we know them.' 'Pôs?' 'Oh come on, Chris,
the plot's thickening deliciously as it is.
Must they be Dutch? Don't worry him! He might
object to what we daydream for tonight...
– Right, Mr Kokkalopoulos!' 'Christos,
call me.' 'We've Greek names too: Christophoros!
and I'm Big Al (Alexandrós the Great);
we're English though.' He offered us a plate
of his Arcadian figs, and we became
his guests, and bound to play a decent game.
'So much
for firming up our unconditioned pricks.
We'd be ashamed to smutch
the honour of his roof: our wicks
will never meet the snuffing Dutch.'

'Sez you,' you said: 'My poker's free of shame.
My wife has left me for an ancient flame;
I'll quench my ardour where I like, and here
I like.' So we walked, arguing, for our gear,
to the main road; back to our concrete shelf
for lunch above the donkey and the Alph;
lay down for half an hour in the rival
kingdom of sleep; but talked of the arrival
of trousered girls. 'O my old Dutch, my old
Dutch cap, where are you now? Come home,' you carolled.
'I was an intellectual carrot, till
you took my bulb in hand.' This narrative thrill
was carrying us away: we'd swim again,
at our age, in the emotions of young men.
I suddenly saw you were no longer pinned
to a position on the chart: the wind
was teasing you to sea, to other ports,
to life without the curse of second thoughts,
to isles and Sirens and the gulfs of loss.

Help, god of Friendship! 'O Christophoros,
let's go and see the castro.' (Surely a wrecked
building will calm a lustful architect.)

It loured, mauled by the clumsy hand of time,
an outdoor art-work. We began to climb,
and I was soon regretting my lost boots –
a big black snake slid out from stones and roots,
glanced at my naked ankles and writhed off,
flickering. I can't touch a photograph
of a snake, let alone brave a real snake.
Was it for shame or maybe friendship's sake
that I kept climbing? or feeling I was stuck
firm on a line of guaranteed good luck,
the curve of confidence which everyone
follows towards inevitable fun.

Kolokotronis must have stood here, hoping
to hold the castle, and rebuilt this coping
with gaps for cannon. Byron used to say,
'Don't trust the Franks to get you freedom – they
live in the distance and can go away.'
These Frankish walls, however, nobly stayed,
one bonus from the evil Fourth Crusade.
Kolokotronis must have loved it here –
after the draftier and draftier
hillsides, this barrack would have seemed a palace,
with a non-stop arc of fire on the police,
I mean the Turks, and comfortable hours
of warning. Like my Border ancestors
in Liddesdale, these brigands studied views:
grand prospects have a military use.
They must have drunk nothing but wine and rain:
the river's
a thousand feet below us,
running towards Olympia's
race-tracks, and Arethusa's
melting Sicilian embrace.

'Thirsty?' We get down to the road again.
A car goes by but stops. Inside the two
Dutch girls (who did they recognize, me or you? –
they knew my hat) and Kokkalopoulos' sister-

in-law and brother: they've all been to Mystra.
We pack in, close. I'm nearly sitting on
the one I like, the rounder prettier one.
The story's going too fast to understand –
I've met her thigh before I've touched her hand.

Back at the house, over a drink, we offer
our names, and Athanasios and Martha
concentrate on your surname, which you quote as
Curt-Hose, a friend of Goulielmos Protos.
I have been calling you (from Milton) 'Crowtoes':
they turn you into Kondopandelonakis.
The conversation can't get worse than this,
and does get better: Christos tells us he's a
hard-worked shepherd; his brother's life is easy
in Athens, trading old English pianos.
It seems that nobody in Bolton knows
how good their pianos are – in Lancashire
they want (like overcoats not made of fur)
some electronic instrument from Japan –
in Attica though, this witty businessman
imports them for the Athenian bourgeoisie.
'I do it all by phone, no sweat.' 'How many?'
'About five hundred.'
                                        The Kokkalopouli
are giving the Dutch girls dinner, but not us.
We eat down in the square, where we discuss
souvlakia and Marinka and Annette,
disputing which was which (for I forget),
wondering if they share the interest
you burn with. 'I should think we're just a pest.
Surely girls are lovely to one another,
and fold together peaceably without bother.
If I were in their skin that's what I'd do.'
'You lazy sod! Thank God I'm not like you.
You think they're Lesbians? – Anyway, I'll convert them.
If not, my boneless finger won't have hurt them.'
Not that you were a selfish ram: you were
a bursting-bollocked sad grass-widower
whose wife was spending six months with the tool
of an old love recalled from dancing-school.

When you could face the girls without attack-
ing their closed zips and buttons, we went back.
The moon on the terrace buttered everything white
on one side: we were dark, the Dutch girls bright
across the table, with the Greeks. We eight
sat in the silver, drinking. Among the wet
Olympic rings of wine I wrote a lady's
name on the wood invisibly. Christos played his
pastoral flute for us and for his wife.
They went to bed. We stayed to talk of Life.
Martha, who teaches literature, now finds
that I'm a poet: winning hearts and minds
for the good cause? what do I write about?
Not politics: I live in amorous doubt
among the lovely policies and can't tell
which good intentions will not lead to hell.
There in the black/white moonlit Peloponnese
she recommends Plekhanov's theories;
Karl Kautsky; and the two best novelists known in
her circle, Tolstoy (A.) and A.J. Cronin.
I thank her – she is charming and sincere –
but say I follow Homer, for it's clear
he has no favourites in the *Iliad*:
he never says Greeks Good, or Asians Bad –
his subject's *anger*; his impartial art
covers the partialities of the heart.
The enemy isn't classes, tribes, or creeds –
the enemy is universal needs.
Remember Diomedes spears the goddess
of love, the inner enemy of our bodies;
he tears her sleeve, the ichor in a stream
pours from her fragile wrist: he's made her scream;
and then he stabs the god of war, and where?
the lower belly, Aphrodite's care,
the hinge of Yin and Yang – but now I find
I'm flying off the point; she's left behind,
so I cite Palamas, who also shirks
the job of telling how a good state works.
'He sings
of nakedness, and can you tell
from other clues among his writings
what policy he was trying to sell –
except a Gypsy's view of things?'

To her, this is the Treason of the Clerks:
writers should teach the people how to vote –
in verse, I ask, in verse? Her husband wrote
short stories... Did he feel the same about
his readers? Maybe I'd begun to shout
(having no opinions strengthens the emotions):
disturbed and bored, the girls were making motions
toward their room. O Christopher, the prey
was up: in seconds they'd have got away.
Infected, we yawned too. In seconds, we
were whispering from the narrow balcony,
come see our room, come chat, come socialize
in the deep sense of strangers meeting eyes,
sharing the breath of words. So near your skin
you soon know what one wants: mine was the thin
unhappy older one from somewhere by
Rotterdam, and she wanted nobody.
The silence pushed our words apart: a thought,
'Don't wake the donkey', muscled through unsought.
Your words were warmer but no happier; soon
we all fled singly to the primal swoon,
forgetting the spongy buttock of the moon.

We never saw the girls again. Next day
they slept in, tactful, or worn out with play.
Christos, up early, had the luck to chase
and catch a wild goat in a narrow place
among the rocks. He milked it, so we had
warm wild-goat's milk with his wife's bread. Not bad,
I told him; but I think the kick was all
in the idea – the taste I can't recall.
I must have said to Athanasios
this milk might be a poem; or the loss
of my brown boots – 'Your what?' 'His kaphé botès.'
(I thought, the northern daydream, coffee bodies...)
He kindly phoned the ministry of found
objects (things in the way or lying round),
but they were vague. He drove us to the bus
stop in the town, but some mysterious
message – he sat there silent at the wheel,
the villagers at tin tables frozen still –
told him there'd be no bus; and took us further,
to Megalopolis. Christos and Martha

were with us too. I felt like kissing her
when she said, 'Cultured people' (in my ear)
'lose things.' My brown boots! And she tried to give us
another poem, claiming *Eohippus*
was first discovered in the fossil lake
between us and the mountains – a mistake,
I thought, the horse of dawn's American,
a fact unwelcome to a left-wing woman.
Thank God, I didn't say it. For a host
you smile and swallow what repels you most,
a half-cooked eye, an error, or a lie.

At Megalopolis we embraced: Goodbye,
they said; Yassas, we cried, and felt alone
like two old boots, abandoned, on our own.

As we sat waiting in the dusty Aithousa
for the next bus, I thought of the next user
of my dear coffee-boots. I hoped it would
be someone oribatic, wild, and good,
someone as rough and honest as the rock,
who played a natural music to his flock.

Everywhere by the little roads of Greece
you see laid out, as landmarks for the bees,
their pale-blue-painted hives, like cubic flowers
to which they bring the sweets of sunny hours.
Such quiet purposes, composed in rings,
console us for the bitter loss of things.

That night we slept at Sparta, capital
of cuckoldry; and dreamed, in the Hotel
Menelaion, of chasing antique ladies
in and out of the peristyles of Hades:
for here Alexandrós, the shepherd boy
and son of Priam, caused the fall of Troy
by stealing
the loveliest woman known.
Had she the gift of healing
the pangs of love? Were his boots brown?
I woke up early, feeling

we had escaped into a world of joy.
I called across the room: 'Chris, she came back.
He had to give her up, so she went back.
Philoctetes killed him and they brought her back.
Menelaus looked at her and took her back.'
So we went down for breakfast on our feet
in the Dioscuri Bar on Old-Word Street.

A Nice Old Word

for T.H.

Some of us drove to Arachova, to eat
at Kyria Panagiotis' flame-lit cave:
tables muffled with rugs, a long stone seat
part of the wall: a comfy hero's grave,
an underworld of thickly padded stone.

The old woman served us lamb and parboiled grasses,
dimly. Arachova vanished. We were alone
in the cell of space, tasting cheese from Parnassus,
made by shepherds, kept in unmelting snows,
the luscious salted crust of yoghurt, wine
trodden by friends, by everyone she knows.

She comes, raising her hand as if to sign
a blessing, but with the awe of a new lover
strokes Ndonis' cheek: 'Hapalos, hapalos,'
she whispers. We all blush as she turns over
unmelted meanings: in our memories
a word for 'maidens', with a pencilled gloss
buried now in our school Euripides.

The Trashtí

Everyone called him the *trashtí*, a name
conceived somewhere between our languages.
Speechless, perhaps an outcast, he would come
at lucky intervals of seven days,
pushing his metal wheelbarrow, which was always
smouldering, ready to stick out tongues of flame,
loaded with all our neighbours' rubbish. We
poured ours on, gave a few coins, and he'd roll away,

bent, in a whirl of smoke, the fire reducing
our week's waste to a reminiscent glow,
an iris-out of history. It was surprising
he needed nothing else, no other vehicle,
no dumping-ground, no help. For all we knew
he was outdoing Hercules, by cleansing
the whole city – but seemed too dim and slow,
in a robe thrown away centuries ago.

We fill two dustbins now, one each. I recall
walking from Bagh-e-Sheikh, cold in the early light,
to queue for *nan* at the breadshop in the wall,
and bringing it home draped on my forearm, hot
still from the oven. Apples-of-earth and carrots
were bought unwrapped too, yoghurt in a bowl
which you took back. Our garbage must have been peel
and tea-leaves, envelopes, fruit-pips, bones and eggshells,

some pages of *Kayhan*, and the paper on the *mast*
(the yoghurt). Now I think we need that man,
the *trashtí*, to come back, to make our dust
weigh less than us, before the dumps advance
like lava, a layer the sun's too weak to cleanse,
of substances no creature can digest.
But is he dead? Or does a bonfire still
wobble around Shiraz on one bad wheel?

Ablutions in Cambridge

My dear friend, we are old:
not to ourselves, but to the perfect judges
who stand well-licked and slender – and unwrinkled.
I think our relatively unemployed
beauties offend their palate:
they are embarrassed by our long-kept juices.

When you went down to wash
among your daughter's friends, among the mirrors
and lines of radiating water, your marked flesh –
or something pensive in the way your eyes
passed, or even did not pass,
over their exhilarating simple figures –

abashed them, as if you'd sprouted
the complacent little nozzle of a male.
They hid in steam; or in cold showers cavorted
without the shrieks of waking. But were they shown
the inhabitant of your old dressing-gown?
Did you give them a chance to sigh or smile?

I think not. It was early,
too early to confront the powers of time,
or to recall the world is not entirely
in quick-reacting youthful hands.
You splashed discreetly; they looked away; not a hint
of a revolution crossed the cloudy room.

An Old Theory of Vision

How do I see you? You are over there
casually scratching your unimprovable neck
with your left hand: your image comes through the air
inexhaustibly, as long as I can look,
and visible from the door, the floor, this chair.

Lucretius would have said you were casting off
a film of skin, one coat of molecules,
like a mayfly's exoskeleton, a snake's slough;
that what I see is an ecdysis of veils,
things stripping themselves of infinitesimal stuff.

'So thin they don't get in each other's way' –
too thin to kiss – these simulacra peel
and float away, all over. We might say
things would wear down to nothing; all that foil
would stifle us – unless it could decay.

'Most of it does – but sometimes some remains,
the old look of a person. That's a ghost.'
Oh comfortable theory, that explains
I may still see you when your body's lost –
longer, more often, and without such pains.

Meanwhile the photons come and go between us
without confusion, taking images
for rides, to where there may be retinas
or not, with minds to read the touching messages –
delivered upside-down and from a distance.

Seeing Things

Late afternoon on the prairie. We were looking
for birds. My old friend Michael was amazed
at what we said we saw: such far-off dots,
how could we pick them out? still less remark,
'Eastern *and* western kingbirds.' We all three
wore specs. 'You must have great peripheral vision,'
he finally pronounced – as if we scanned
the field like radar with a sensitive edge,
as if we spotted things by accident,
out of the corner of a thoughtless eye.
We tried to say that knowing where to look
we saw things: where they were, one other detail
might be enough to name them; we were finding,
in the pink light, what we knew might be there.
I don't think he believed us.

Then this summer
in England by some oaks and poplar trees
I stood still in a field while swifts were picking
invisible insects from the flow of air.
To them I was a post: their eyes were focused
and fixed on space some yards ahead of them,
to catch a thousand flies an hour. They leave
the bees and take the stingless drones. They scream
with their mouths full – and when they sighted me
I was the distance of a fly away:
the target distance. Then they swerved aside,
seeing obstruction.

They can change the focus,
of course. When they migrate, to see the map
below, they focus on infinity.

And we can focus on nothing, as I do now,
to think of how we looked at Robert's farm.

Turnstones on Lewis

Pale in the shade of a taller person
I have seen these birds before;
in the wintry black and white
of my father's telescope
I used to watch them turning
the stones and spinachy weed,
guest-workers from the north
with an international job.

They search for something to eat,
the soft stuff lying under
uncompromising hardness
in the wet space between languages
where solid and liquid fret;
they ask only for stones
to hide among and hunt in,
and dipterans (they love midges).

Today their colours show
for once, the tortoiseshell
feathers of summer. The birds
pose for a moment, characterless.
What are they? I don't know,
forgetting even the word
turnstone. The manual tells me:
Arenaria interpres –

they are translators of stones,
turners of words, probers
of worn old surfaces
for meanings that live here
in the white fragmented-bone
shell-sand of the Hebrides,
a calcium of lost shapes
that will be eggs next year.

The Last Speaker

I remember that meeting of the Modern Language
Association, not because there were cowboys –
who turned out to be interpreters of James Joyce
or dab hands at the Platonic Relevance Sandwich –
but because of the parrot auctioned the last day.

This bird, a gloomy figure in blue and green,
stuck a black tongue out, the sole surviving organ
of an Amazonian tribe, its prose and poetry.

But while bidding proceeded, with nods, and swishes
of programmes, and plaintive calls of sacred numbers
in all the dialects of American riches,
the bird stood motionless, unpromising, empty,
till silence came.
                                        As the hammer rose, it spoke
The Creation, learned in the long-house for a joke.

Rilke's Posthumous Sonnet to Orpheus

You swallow the delighted air. You lift
Your pipe towards the hesitating trees:
So used to holy living on their knees
They fear to move. But blossom whispers, 'Drift!',

And all the animals begin to sing
Before you give a note, as if the word
Eurydice spoke last could still be heard,
Echoing in the cells of every Thing.

And stones in circles leave their beds and walk.
Rivers climb mountains for a better view.

The stars turn back and listen. The First Cause
Sits up and signs to Chaos not to talk.

Sweet Orpheus, don't stop singing: if you do,
The end of everything will be Applause.

Ganning Back to the Beginning

for Martin and Diana

I

HWAET! This is what we   wanted to hear:

The floating one swings   still among rocks,
hovering on hemp,   the embracing boat
fast at anchor.   The coastguard on horse-back
guides them to Heorot   the shining hall –
the loom of it lightens   the heart of sailors.
They bend to sit   on a bench, a bank,
the modelled metal   in plates and rings
works on their bodies,   distinctive creaking.
Their leader stands,   the proud words flash
from the fire-hard helmet: 'We synt Higelaces
beodgeneatas;   Beowulf is min nama.'

II

The hall in the story,   the hall of man,
rings with rapture.   We have been waiting
for years for this.
                              Glaedman Davies,
as I chew the words   of Anon's masterpiece,
I read yours too,   in your manuscript notebook
the faithful trot.   The date there drops me
back where you wrote it,   the room in the roof
above my head   with no view of the quad,
no view of girls,   the wound-givers
in light armour,   distinctly creaking:
they would open their wordhoards   under my windows,
on the red gravel,   while you read and plucked
these words from a glossary   and I turned blindly
to Aristotle prosing   on the kinds of friendship.

III

That was Healfdene's Hall, the House of Housman,
the lane of light where on lines of benches
scholars feast and warriors wait
with towels on shield-arms for the words of grace.